Presented To:

_____

By:

_____

Date:

_____

GOD'S LITTLE INSTRUCTION BOOK
VOLUMES I · II · III

God's Little Instruction Book, Volumes I · II · III
ISBN 1-56292-468-0
Copyright © 1997 by Honor Books, Inc.
P. O. Box 55388
Tulsa, OK 74155

Introduction

The three-volume *God's Little Instruction Book Series* is a collection of inspirational quotes and scriptures designed to motivate you to live a meaningful, productive, and happy life.

The original was first published in 1993. Little did we know then how popular it would become! Now printed in 15 foreign languages, it has sold more than a million copies. The two sequels continued the tradition of bringing you inspiration and challenge to lift your sights and spirit.

Now the wisdom, encouragement, and humor of all three books are available to you in this one handsome volume. *God's Little Instruction Book I · II · III* is sure to become one of the most treasured books in your library!

A word fitly spoken is like apples of gold in settings of silver.
(Proverbs 25:11 NKJV)

GOD'S LITTLE INSTRUCTION BOOK I

A marriage may be made in heaven, but the maintenance must be done on earth.

9

Nevertheless let every one of you in particular so love his wife even as himself; and the wife see that she reverence her husband.
Ephesians 5:33

When God measures a man, He puts the
tape around the heart instead of the head.

*The LORD seeth not as man seeth; for man looketh on
the outward appearance, but the LORD looketh on the heart.*
1 Samuel 16:7

10

The grass may look greener on the other side,
but it still has to be mowed.

And be content with such things as ye have.
Hebrews 13:5

Patience is the ability to keep your motor idling when you feel like stripping your gears.

11

He that is slow to anger is better than the mighty;
and he that ruleth his spirit than he that taketh a city.
Proverbs 16:32

He who is waiting for something to turn up might start with his own shirt sleeves.

All hard work brings a profit, but mere talk leads only to poverty.
Proverbs 14:23 NIV

❧

12 Remember the banana — when it left the bunch, it got skinned.

Not forsaking the assembling of ourselves together,
as the manner of some is; but exhorting one another:
and so much the more, as ye see the day approaching.
Hebrews 10:25

It is better to be silent and be considered a fool than to speak and remove all doubt.

13

Yea also, when he that is a fool walketh by the way,
his wisdom faileth him, and he saith to every one that he is a fool.
Ecclesiastes 10:3

Many a good man has failed because he had his wishbone where his backbone should have been.

Have not I commanded thee? Be strong and of a good courage; be not afraid, neither be thou dismayed: for the LORD thy God is with thee whithersoever thou goest.
Joshua 1:9

14

If at first you don't succeed, try reading the instructions.

Take fast hold of instruction; let her not go: keep her; for she is thy life.
Proverbs 4:13

Your temper is like a fire. It gets very destructive when it gets out of control.

15

*He that hath no rule over his own spirit is like
a city that is broken down, and without walls.*
Proverbs 25:28

Decisions can take you out of God's will
but never out of His reach.

If we are faithless, he will remain faithful, for he cannot disown himself.
2 Timothy 2:13 NIV

16

Your companions are like
the buttons on an elevator. They will either
take you up or they will take you down.

He that walketh with wise men shall be wise:
but a companion of fools shall be destroyed.
Proverbs 13:20

Patience is a quality you admire in the driver behind you and scorn in the one ahead.

17

The end of a matter is better than its beginning,
and patience is better than pride. Do not be quickly provoked
in your spirit, for anger resides in the lap of fools.
Ecclesiastes 7:8,9 NIV

There is a name for people who are not
excited about their work — unemployed.

And whatsoever ye do, do it heartily, as to the Lord, and not unto men.
Colossians 3:23

❧

A person's true character is revealed by
what he does when no one is watching.

Obey them not only to win their favor when their eye is on you,
but like slaves of Christ, doing the will of God from your heart.
Ephesians 6:6 NIV

It's better to die with a good name than to live with a bad one.

19

A good name is better than precious ointment.
Ecclesiastes 7:1

"No" is one of the few words
that can never be misunderstood.

But let your statement be, "Yes, yes" or "No, no."
Matthew 5:37 NASB

20

Too many churchgoers are singing
"Standing on the Promises" when all they
are doing is sitting on the premises.

That ye be not slothful, but followers of them who
through faith and patience inherit the promises.
Hebrews 6:12

Some people complain because God put thorns on roses, while others praise Him for putting roses among thorns.

21

Finally, brethren, whatsoever things are true, whatsoever things are honest, whatsoever things are just, whatsoever things are pure, whatsoever things are lovely, whatsoever things are of good report; if there be any virtue, and if there be any praise, think on these things.
Philippians 4:8

The cure of crime is not in the electric chair, but in the high chair.

Train up a child in the way he should go:
and when he is old, he will not depart from it.
Proverbs 22:6

22

The bridge you burn now may be the one you later have to cross.

If it be possible, as much as lieth in you, live peaceably with all men.
Romans 12:18

The measure of a man is not how great his faith is but how great his love is.

23

And now these three remain: faith, hope and love.
But the greatest of these is love.
1 Corinthians 13:13 NIV

Real friends are those who,
when you've made a fool of yourself,
don't feel you've done a permanent job.

Beareth all things, believeth all things, hopeth all things,
endureth all things. Charity never faileth.
1 Corinthians 13:7,8

24

Be careful that your marriage doesn't
become a duel instead of a duet.

Let us therefore follow after the things which make for peace,
and things wherewith one may edify another.
Romans 14:19

The mighty oak was once a little nut that stood its ground.

25

A man shall not be established by wickedness:
but the root of the righteous shall not be moved.
Proverbs 12:3

The secret of achievement is
to not let what you're doing
get to you before you get to it.

Commit thy works unto the LORD, and thy thoughts shall be established.
Proverbs 16:3

Most people wish to serve God — but only
in an advisory capacity.

Humble yourselves therefore under the mighty hand of God,
that he may exalt you in due time.
1 Peter 5:6

Conscience is God's built-in warning system. Be very happy when it hurts you. Be very worried when it doesn't. [27]

And herein do I exercise myself, to have always a conscience void of offense toward God, and toward men.
Acts 24:16

Most men forget God all day and ask
Him to remember them at night.

*Evening, and morning, and at noon, will I pray,
and cry aloud: and he shall hear my voice.*
Psalm 55:17

28

If you don't stand for something
you'll fall for anything!

If you do not stand firm in your faith, you will not stand at all.
Isaiah 7:9 NIV

The measure of a man's character
is not what he gets
from his ancestors, but what
he leaves his descendants.

29

A good man leaveth an inheritance to his children's children:
and the wealth of the sinner is laid up for the just.
Proverbs 13:22

Although the tongue weighs very little,
few people are able to hold it.

Even so the tongue is a little member, and boasteth great things.
Behold, how great a matter a little fire kindleth!
James 3:5

30

You should never let adversity
get you down — except on your knees.

Is any one of you in trouble? He should pray.
James 5:13 NIV

He who wants milk should not
sit on a stool in the middle
of the pasture expecting
the cow to back up to him.

He becometh poor that dealeth with a slack hand:
but the hand of the diligent maketh rich.
Proverbs 10:4

The best bridge between hope and despair is often a good night's sleep.

It is vain for you to rise up early, to sit up late, to eat the bread of sorrows: for so he giveth his beloved sleep.
Psalm 127:2

32

It is good to remember that the teakettle, although up to its neck in hot water, continues to sing.

Rejoice evermore. In every thing give thanks: for this is the will of God in Christ Jesus concerning you.
1 Thessalonians 5:16,18

It's good to be a Christian and know it, but it's better to be a Christian and show it!

33

By this shall all men know that ye are my disciples, if ye have love one to another.
John 13:35

Sorrow looks back. Worry looks around.
Faith looks up.

*Fixing our eyes on Jesus, the author and perfecter of faith,
who for the joy set before Him endured the cross, despising the shame,
and has sat down at the right hand of the throne of God.*
Hebrews 12:2 NASB

34

A man is never in worse company than
when he flies into a rage and is beside himself.

He that is soon angry dealeth foolishly.
Proverbs 14:17

Success in marriage is more
than finding the right person.
It's becoming the right person.

35

But thou, O man of God, flee these things; and follow after
righteousness, godliness, faith, love, patience, meekness.
1 Timothy 6:11

Failure in people is caused more by
lack of determination than lack in talent.

And let us not be weary in well doing:
for in due season we shall reap, if we faint not.
Galatians 6:9

A man is rich according to what he *is*,
not according to what he *has*.

There is that maketh himself rich, yet hath nothing:
there is that maketh himself poor, yet hath great riches.
Proverbs 13:7

Life can only be understood by looking backward, but it must be lived by looking forward.

37

And Jesus said unto him, No man, having put his hand to the plough, and looking back, is fit for the kingdom of God.
Luke 9:62

Success comes in cans;
failure comes in can'ts.

I can do all things through Christ which strengtheneth me.
Philippians 4:13

❧

Sometimes we are so busy adding up
our troubles that we forget to
count our blessings.

I will remember the works of the LORD: surely I will remember thy
wonders of old. I will meditate also of all thy work, and talk of thy doings.
Psalm 77:11,12

38

Falling down doesn't make you a failure, but staying down does.

39

For a just man falleth seven times, and riseth up again.
Proverbs 24:16

If a task is once begun, never leave it
'till it's done. Be the labor great or small,
do it well or not at all.

I have glorified thee on the earth:
I have finished the work which thou gavest me to do.
John 17:4

40

Time is more valuable than money
because time is irreplaceable.

Redeeming the time, because the days are evil.
Ephesians 5:16

The best way to forget your own problems is to help someone solve his.

Look not every man on his own things,
but every man also on the things of others.
Philippians 2:4

41

God can heal a broken heart, but He has to have all the pieces.

My son, give me thine heart.
Proverbs 23:26

42

Authority makes some people grow — and others just swell.

But he that is greatest among you shall be your servant.
And whosoever shall exalt himself shall be abased;
and he that shall humble himself shall be exalted.
Matthew 23:11,12

Be more concerned with what God thinks about you than what people think about you.

43

Then Peter and the other apostles answered and said,
We ought to obey God rather than men.
Acts 5:29

The trouble with the guy who talks too fast is that he often says something he hasn't thought of yet.

Be not rash with thy mouth, and let not thine heart
be hasty to utter any thing before God: for God is in heaven,
and thou upon earth: therefore let thy words be few.
Ecclesiastes 5:2

44

The best way to get the last word is to apologize.

If you have been trapped by what you said, ensnared by the words
of your mouth, then do this, my son, to free yourself, since you have
fallen into your neighbor's hands: Go and humble yourself;
press your plea with your neighbor!
Proverbs 6:2,3 NIV

The train of failure usually runs on the track of laziness.

By much slothfulness the building decayeth; and through idleness of the hands the house droppeth through.
Ecclesiastes 10:18

When confronted with a Goliath-sized problem,
which way do you respond: "He's too big to hit"
or, like David, "He's too big to miss"?

*The LORD that delivered me out of the paw of the lion, and out of the
paw of the bear, he will deliver me out of the hand of this Philistine.*
1 Samuel 17:37

46

Forget yourself for others and
others will not forget you!

*Therefore all things whatsoever ye would that men should do to you,
do ye even so to them: for this is the law and the prophets.*
Matthew 7:12

The secret of success is to start from scratch and keep on scratching.

47

*And the seed in the good soil, these are the ones
who have heard the word in an honest and good heart,
and hold it fast, and bear fruit with perseverance.*
Luke 8:15 NASB

The secret of contentment is the realization that life is a gift not a right.

But godliness with contentment is great gain.
For we brought nothing into this world,
and it is certain we can carry nothing out.
1 Timothy 6:6,7

48

No one ever said on their deathbed:
I wish I would have spent more time at work!

Yea, I hated all my labour which I had taken under the sun:
because I should leave it unto the man that shall be after me.
Ecclesiastes 2:18

True faith and courage are like a kite — an opposing wind raises it higher.

49

But they that wait upon the LORD shall renew their strength; they shall mount up with wings as eagles; they shall run, and not be weary; and they shall walk, and not faint.
Isaiah 40:31

In order to receive the direction from God you must be able to receive the correction from God.

My son, despise not thou the chastening of the Lord,
nor faint when thou art rebuked of him: For whom the Lord loveth
he chasteneth, and scourgeth every son whom he receiveth.
Hebrews 12:5,6

50

Those who bring sunshine to the lives of others cannot keep it from themselves.

Be not deceived; God is not mocked: for whatsoever
a man soweth, that shall he also reap.
Galatians 6:7

No man ever really finds out what he believes in until he begins to instruct his children. 51

And, ye fathers, provoke not your children to wrath:
but bring them up in the nurture and admonition of the Lord.
Ephesians 6:4

The doors of opportunity are marked "Push" and "Pull."

The soul of the sluggard desireth, and hath nothing:
but the soul of the diligent shall be made fat.
Proverbs 13:4

It's the little things in life that determine the big things.

Thou hast been faithful over a few things, I will make thee
ruler over many things: enter thou into the joy of thy lord.
Matthew 25:21

Don't mistake activity for achievement. Busyness does not equal productiveness.

Martha was cumbered about much serving, and came to him, and said, Lord, dost thou not care that my sister hath left me to serve alone?... And Jesus answered and said unto her, Martha, Martha, thou art careful and troubled about many things: But one thing is needful: and Mary hath chosen that good part.

Luke 10:40-42

53

You cannot win if you do not begin.

Now therefore perform the doing of it; that as there was a readiness to will,
so there may be a performance also out of that which ye have.
2 Corinthians 8:11

54

The best way to be successful is to
follow the advice you give others.

He who ignores discipline despises himself,
but whoever heeds correction gains understanding.
Proverbs 15:32 NIV

Contentment isn't getting what we want but being satisfied with what we have.

55

Not that I speak in respect of want: for I have learned, in whatsoever state I am, therewith to be content.
Philippians 4:11

Too many people quit looking for work
when they find a job.

He also that is slothful in his work is
brother to him that is a great waster.
Proverbs 18:9

Ability will enable a man to go to the top,
but it takes character to keep him there.

The righteousness of the blameless makes a straight way for them,
but the wicked are brought down by their own wickedness.
Proverbs 11:5 NIV

You can't take your money with you, but you can send it on ahead.

Lay not up for yourselves treasures upon earth, where moth and rust doth corrupt, and where thieves break through and steal: but lay up for yourselves treasures in heaven, where neither moth nor rust doth corrupt, and where thieves do not break through nor steal.
Matthew 6:19,20

57

Your words are windows to your heart.

Out of the abundance of the heart the mouth speaketh.
Matthew 12:34

58

A shut mouth gathers no foot.

He that keepeth his mouth keepeth his life:
but he that openeth wide his lips shall have destruction.
Proverbs 13:3

The only fool bigger than the person who knows it all is the person who argues with him.

59

He that reproveth a scorner getteth to himself shame:
and he that rebuketh a wicked man getteth himself a blot.
Proverbs 9:7

A drowning man does not complain
about the size of a life preserver.

Do all things without murmurings and disputings.
Philippians 2:14

❧

Blessed is he who, having nothing to say,
refrains from giving wordy evidence of the fact.

The tongue of the wise useth knowledge aright:
but the mouth of fools poureth out foolishness.
Proverbs 15:2

Luck: a loser's excuse for a winner's position.

61

The soul of the sluggard desireth, and hath nothing:
but the soul of the diligent shall be made fat.
Proverbs 13:4

Do the thing you fear and the death of fear is certain.

Be strong and of a good courage, fear not, nor be afraid of them: for the LORD thy God, he it is that doth go with thee; he will not fail thee, nor forsake thee.
Deuteronomy 31:6

62

God plus one is always a majority!

If God be for us, who can be against us?
Romans 8:31

Whoever gossips to you will be a gossip of you.

A talebearer revealeth secrets: but he that is of a faithful spirit concealeth the matter.
Proverbs 11:13

Jesus is a friend who knows all your
faults and still loves you anyway.

But God commendeth his love toward us, in that,
while we were yet sinners, Christ died for us.
Romans 5:8

64

Every person should have a special cemetery lot in
which to bury the faults of friends and loved ones.

And be ye kind one to another, tenderhearted, forgiving one another,
even as God for Christ's sake hath forgiven you.
Ephesians 4:32

Ignorance is always swift to speak.

65

Let every man be swift to hear, slow to speak, slow to wrath.
James 1:19

Learn from others' mistakes rather than making them all yourself.

The way of a fool is right in his own eyes:
but he that hearkeneth unto counsel is wise.
Proverbs 12:15

66

Pick your friends but not to pieces.

A man that beareth false witness against his neighbour
is a maul, and a sword, and a sharp arrow.
Proverbs 25:18

He who throws dirt loses ground.

Wherefore putting away lying, speak every man truth with his neighbour: for we are members one of another.
Ephesians 4:25

You don't have to lie awake nights to succeed —
just stay awake days.

I must work the works of him that sent me, while it is day:
the night cometh, when no man can work.
John 9:4

The first step to wisdom is silence;
the second is listening.

A wise man will hear, and will increase learning;
and a man of understanding shall attain unto wise counsels.
Proverbs 1:5

The greatest possession you have
is the 24 hours directly
in front of you.

There is a time there for every purpose and for every work.
Ecclesiastes 3:17

The most valuable gift you can give another is a good example.

For I have given you an example, that ye should do as I have done to you.
John 13:15

Don't be afraid of pressure. Remember that pressure is what turns a lump of coal into a diamond.

Knowing this, that the trying of your faith worketh patience.
But let patience have her perfect work, that ye may be
perfect and entire, wanting nothing.
James 1:3,4

A minute of thought is worth more than an hour of talk.

71

Set a watch, O LORD, before my mouth; keep the door of my lips.
Psalm 141:3

You can win more friends with your ears
than with your mouth.

Let every man be swift to hear, slow to speak, slow to wrath.
James 1:19

72

It's not the outlook but the uplook that counts.

Looking unto Jesus the author and finisher of our faith.
Hebrews 12:2

Put others before yourself, and you can become a leader among men.

73

But it shall not be so among you: but whosoever will be great among you, let him be your minister; And whosoever will be chief among you, let him be your servant.
Matthew 20:26,27

Feed your faith and your doubts will starve to death.

*But we are not of those who shrink back to destruction,
but of those who have faith to the preserving of the soul.*
Hebrews 10:39 NASB

Never pass up a chance to keep your mouth shut.

Even a fool, when he holdeth his peace, is counted wise:
and he that shutteth his lips is esteemed a man of understanding.
Proverbs 17:28

It isn't hard to make
a mountain out of a molehill.
Just add a little dirt.

Starting a quarrel is like breaching a dam;
so drop the matter before a dispute breaks out.
Proverbs 17:14 NIV

What counts is not the number of hours you put in,
but how much you put in the hours.

Whatsoever thy hand findeth to do, do it with thy might.
Ecclesiastes 9:10

Reputation is made in a moment:
character is built in a lifetime.

My righteousness I hold fast, and will not let it go:
my heart shall not reproach me so long as I live.
Job 27:6

If you feel "dog tired" at night, maybe it's because you "growled" all day!

77

If it be possible, as much as lieth in you,
live peaceably with all men.
Romans 12:18

If you don't want the fruits of sin,
stay out of the devil's orchard.

Abstain from all appearance of evil.
1 Thessalonians 5:22

Our children are like mirrors —
they reflect our attitudes in life.

The just man walketh in his integrity:
his children are blessed after him.
Proverbs 20:7

The art of being a good guest is knowing when to leave.

79

Withdraw thy foot from thy neighbour's house;
lest he be weary of thee, and so hate thee.
Proverbs 25:17

He who cannot forgive breaks the bridge over which he himself must pass.

For if ye forgive men their trespasses,
your heavenly Father will also forgive you.
Matthew 6:14

Jesus is a friend who walks in when the world has walked out.

These things I have spoken unto you, that in me ye might have peace.
In the world ye shall have tribulation: but be of good cheer;
I have overcome the world.
John 16:33

Those who deserve love the least need it the most.

But I say unto you, Love your enemies, bless them that curse you, [81]
do good to them that hate you, and pray for them
which despitefully use you, and persecute you.
Matthew 5:44

Faith is daring the soul to go beyond what the eyes can see.

For we walk by faith, not by sight.
2 Corinthians 5:7

The right angle to approach a difficult problem is the "try-angle."

For with God nothing shall be impossible.
Luke 1:37

The fellow who does things that count doesn't usually stop to count them.

83

Brothers, I do not consider myself yet to have taken hold of it. But one thing I do: Forgetting what is behind and straining toward what is ahead.
Philippians 3:13 NIV

A critical spirit is like poison ivy — it only takes a little contact to spread its poison.

But avoid worldly and empty chatter, for it will lead to further ungodliness, and their talk will spread like gangrene.
2 Timothy 2:16,17 NASB

84

Laziness and poverty are cousins.

Yet a little sleep, a little slumber, a little folding of the hands to sleep: so shall thy poverty come as one that travelleth; and thy want as an armed man.
Proverbs 24:33,34

Language is the expression of thought. Every time you speak, your mind is on parade.

85

A good man out of the good treasure of his heart bringeth forth that which is good; and an evil man out of the evil treasure of his heart bringeth forth that which is evil: for of the abundance of the heart his mouth speaketh.
Luke 6:45

The hardest secret for a man to keep is his opinion of himself.

For I say, through the grace given unto me, to every man that is among you, not to think of himself more highly than he ought to think; but to think soberly, according as God hath dealt to every man the measure of faith.
Romans 12:3

86

He who buries his talent is making a grave mistake.

Neglect not the gift that is in thee.
1 Timothy 4:14

Take care of your character and your reputation will take care of itself.

A good name is rather to be chosen than great riches,
and loving favour rather than silver and gold.
Proverbs 22:1

Even a woodpecker owes his success to
the fact that he uses his head.

But you, keep your head in all situations.
2 Timothy 4:5 NIV

The poorest of all men is not
the man without a cent but
the man without a dream.

Where there is no vision, the people perish.
Proverbs 29:18

You can accomplish more
in one hour with God than
one lifetime without Him.

With God all things are possible.
Matthew 19:26

The only preparation for tomorrow
is the right use of today.

*Take therefore no thought for the morrow: for the morrow shall take
thought for the things of itself. Sufficient unto the day is the evil thereof.*
Matthew 6:34

90

When things go wrong, don't go wrong with them.

Enter not into the path of the wicked, and go not in the way of evil men.
Proverbs 4:14

Two things are hard on the heart — running up stairs and running down people.

91

Let no corrupt communication proceed out of your mouth,
but that which is good to the use of edifying,
that it may minister grace unto the hearers.
Ephesians 4:29

The best way to get even is to forget.

But love ye your enemies, and do good, and lend, hoping for nothing again;
and your reward shall be great, and ye shall be the children of the Highest:
for he is kind unto the unthankful and to the evil.
Luke 6:35

People don't care how much you know until they know how much you care.

Let nothing be done through strife or vainglory; but in lowliness of mind
let each esteem other better than themselves.
Philippians 2:3

Humor is to life what shock absorbers are to automobiles.

93

A merry heart doeth good like a medicine:
but a broken spirit drieth the bones.
Proverbs 17:22

A man wrapped up in himself makes a very small package.

A fool finds no pleasure in understanding
but delights in airing his own opinions.
Proverbs 18:2 NIV

It isn't your position that makes you happy or unhappy, it's your disposition.

But godliness with contentment is great gain. For we brought
nothing into this world, and it is certain we can carry nothing out.
1 Timothy 6:6,7

It takes more to plow a field than merely turning it over in your mind.

Work with your hands, just as we commanded you; so that you may behave properly toward outsiders and not be in any need.
1 Thessalonians 4:11,12 NASB

Men are like fish. Neither would get into trouble if they kept their mouths shut.

Whoso keepeth his mouth and his tongue keepeth his soul from troubles.
Proverbs 21:23

The heart of a man cannot be determined by the size of his pocketbook.

For what shall it profit a man, if he shall gain the whole world,
and lose his own soul? Or what shall a man give in exchange for his soul?
Mark 8:36,37

Kindness is the oil that takes the friction out of life.

97

But the fruit of the Spirit is...kindness.
Galatians 5:22 NIV

You can easily determine the caliber of
a person by the amount of opposition
it takes to discourage him.

If thou faint in the day of adversity, thy strength is small.
Proverbs 24:10

People know what you are by
what they see, not by what they hear.

Let your light so shine before men, that they may see your good works,
and glorify your Father which is in heaven.
Matthew 5:16

People who try to whittle you down are only trying to reduce you to their size.

99

Blessed are ye, when men shall hate you...and shall reproach you...for the Son of man's sake. Rejoice ye in that day, and leap for joy: for, behold, your reward is great in heaven.
Luke 6:22,23

Quite often when a man thinks his mind is getting broader, it's only his conscience stretching.

Unto the pure all things are pure: but unto them that are defiled and unbelieving is nothing pure; but even their mind and conscience is defiled.
Titus 1:15

100

Temper is what gets most of us into trouble. Pride is what keeps us there.

Pride goeth before destruction, and an haughty spirit before a fall.
Better it is to be of an humble spirit with the lowly,
than to divide the spoil with the proud.
Proverbs 16:18,19

We make a living by what we get — we make a life by what we give.

101

I have shewed you all things, how that so labouring ye ought to support the weak, and to remember the words of the Lord Jesus, how he said, It is more blessed to give than to receive.
Acts 20:35

Our days are identical suitcases —
all the same size — but some people can
pack more into them than others.

Be very careful, then, how you live — not as unwise but as wise,
making the most of every opportunity.
Ephesians 5:15,16 NIV

102

Living would be easier if men showed as much
patience at home as they do when they're fishing.

You husbands likewise, live with your wives in an understanding way.
1 Peter 3:7 NASB

Some people succeed
because they are destined to,
but most people succeed
because they are determined to.

103

And having done all, to stand. Stand therefore....
Ephesians 6:13,14

To forgive is to set a prisoner free and discover the prisoner was YOU.

For if ye forgive men their trespasses, your heavenly Father will also forgive you: But if ye forgive not men their trespasses, neither will your Father forgive your trespasses.
Matthew 6:14,15

104

The company you keep will determine the trouble you meet.

Make no friendship with an angry man; and with a furious man thou shalt not go: lest thou learn his ways, and get a snare to thy soul.
Proverbs 22:24,25

Too many parents are not on spanking terms with their children.

105

He who spares his rod hates his son,
but he who loves him disciplines him diligently.
Proverbs 13:24 NASB

Man cannot discover new oceans unless
he has the courage to lose sight of the shore.

*And Peter answered him and said, Lord, if it be thou, bid me come unto thee
on the water. And he said, Come. And when Peter was come down
out of the ship, he walked on the water, to go to Jesus.
Matthew 14:28,29*

106

The heart is the happiest when
it beats for others.

*Greater love hath no man than this,
that a man lay down his life for his friends.
John 15:13*

One thing you can learn by watching the clock is that it passes time by keeping its hands busy.

107

He also that is slothful in his work is brother
to him that is a great waster.
Proverbs 18:9

Now there's even a "dial-a-prayer" for atheists.
You call a number and nobody answers.

The fool hath said in his heart, There is no God.
Psalm 14:1

108

He who thinks by the inch and talks
by the yard deserves to be kicked by the foot.

A fool's lips bring him strife, and his mouth invites a beating.
Proverbs 18:6 NIV

The best inheritance a father can leave his children is a good example.

109

As ye know how we exhorted and comforted and charged every one of you, as a father doth his children.
1 Thessalonians 2:11

God intervenes in the affairs of men
by invitation only.

*Behold, I stand at the door, and knock: if any man hear my voice, and
open the door, I will come in to him, and will sup with him, and he with me.*
Revelation 3:20

110

If a care is too small to be turned into a prayer,
it is too small to be made into a burden.

Casting all your care upon him; for he careth for you.
1 Peter 5:7

GOD'S LITTLE INSTRUCTION BOOK II

Choice, not chance, determines human destiny.

I have set before you life and death, blessing and cursing: therefore choose life, that both thou and thy seed may live.
Deuteronomy 30:19

The greatest act of faith is when man decides he is not God.

Know ye that the LORD he is God: it is he that hath made us, and not we ourselves; we are his people, and the sheep of his pasture.
Psalm 100:3

Success is to be measured not so much by the position that one has reached in life as by the obstacles which he has overcome while trying to succeed.

Blessed is the man who perseveres under trial, because when he has stood the test, he will receive the crown of life that God has promised to those who love him.
James 1:12 NIV

To be upset over what you don't have is to waste what you do have.

115

Because the Lord is my Shepherd, I have everything I need!
Psalm 23:1 TLB

A true friend never gets in your way
unless you happen to be going down.

A friend loves at all times, and a brother is born for adversity.
Proverbs 17:17 NASB

Laughter is the brush that sweeps away
the cobwebs of the heart.

A happy heart is good medicine and a cheerful mind works healing,
but a broken spirit dries up the bones.
Proverbs 17:22 AMP

Many a man thinks he has an open mind, when it's merely vacant.

117

*I warn everyone among you not to estimate
and think of himself more highly than he ought
[not to have an exaggerated opinion of his own importance].*
Romans 12:3 AMP

Character is not made in crisis, it is only exhibited.

*I have set the LORD always before me:
because he is at my right hand, I shall not be moved.
Psalm 16:8*

118 Swallowing angry words before you say them is better than having to eat them afterwards.

*From the fruit of his mouth a man's stomach is filled;
with the harvest from his lips he is satisfied. The tongue has
the power of life and death, and those who love it will eat its fruit.
Proverbs 18:20,21 NIV*

Happiness is a perfume you cannot pour on others without getting a few drops on yourself.

119

Happy are those who long to be just and good,
for they shall be completely satisfied.
Matthew 5:6 TLB

Wisdom is the quality that keeps you from getting into situations where you need it.

*I would have you learn this great fact: that a life of doing right
is the wisest life there is. If you live that kind of life,
you'll not limp or stumble as you run.*
Proverbs 4:11,12 TLB

120

Rank does not confer privilege or give power. It imposes responsibility.

*For everyone to whom much is given, of him shall much be required;
and of him to whom men entrust much, they will require
and demand all the more.*
Luke 12:48 AMP

God has a history of using the insignificant to accomplish the impossible.

121

And Jesus looking upon them saith, With men it is impossible, but not with God: for with God all things are possible.
Mark 10:27

Depend on it, God's work done in
God's way will never lack God's supplies.

If you are willing and obedient, you will eat the best from the land.
Isaiah 1:19 NIV

122

It's not how many hours you put in
but how much you put into the hours.

Whatever you do, work at it with all your heart, as working for the Lord,
not for men....It is the Lord Christ you are serving.
Colossians 3:23,24 NIV

A skeptic is a person who, when he sees the handwriting on the wall, claims it is a forgery. 123

The fool hath said in his heart, There is no God.
Psalm 14:1

Two things are bad for the heart —
running up stairs and running down people.

Let no corrupt communication proceed out of your mouth,
but that which is good to the use of edifying,
that it may minister grace unto the hearers.
Ephesians 4:29

124

The trouble with most of us is that we would
rather be ruined by praise than saved by criticism.

If you profit from constructive criticism you will be elected to
the wise men's hall of fame. But to reject criticism is to
harm yourself and your own best interests.
Proverbs 15:31,32 TLB

People may doubt what you say, but they will always believe what you do.

125

The tree is known and recognized and judged by its fruit.
Matthew 12:33 AMP

A professional is someone who can do his best work when he doesn't feel like it.

To win the contest you must deny yourselves many things that would keep you from doing your best.
1 Corinthians 9:25 TLB

126

For peace of mind, resign as general manager of the universe.

Cease striving and know that I am God.
Psalm 46:10 NASB

The best inheritance
a parent can give to
his children is a few minutes
of his time each day.

Be very careful, then, how you live — not as unwise
but as wise, making the most of every opportunity.
Ephesians 5:15,16 NIV

No one is useless in this world who lightens the burden of anyone else.

*Now we who are strong ought to bear the weaknesses of
those without strength and not just please ourselves.
Let each of us please his neighbor for his good, to his edification.*
Romans 15:1,2 NASB

Anger is a stone thrown at a wasp's nest.

*Do not be quick in spirit to be angry or vexed,
for anger and vexation lodge in the bosom of fools.*
Ecclesiastes 7:9 AMP

Wisdom is the wealth of the wise.

For the value of wisdom is far above rubies;
nothing can be compared with it.
Proverbs 8:11 TLB

If you want to be a leader with
a large following, just obey the speed limit
on a winding, two-lane road.

*Everyone has heard about your obedience, so I am full of joy over you; but
I want you to be wise about what is good, and innocent about what is evil.*
Romans 16:19 NIV

130

Urgent things are seldom important.
Important things are seldom urgent.

Every prudent man dealeth with knowledge.
Proverbs 13:16

Kindness is a language which the deaf can hear and the blind can see.

131

For his merciful kindness is great toward us: and the truth of the LORD endureth for ever. Praise ye the LORD.
Psalm 117:2

People will be more impressed by the depth of your conviction than the height of your logic.

My son, forget not my law; but let thine heart keep my commandments.... So shalt thou find favour and good understanding in the sight of God and man.
Proverbs 3:1,4

132

The most disappointed people in the world are those who get what is coming to them.

A man's own folly ruins his life, yet his heart rages against the LORD.
Proverbs 19:3 NIV

Life affords no greater responsibility, no greater privilege, than the raising of the next generation.

133

Teach them (God's commandments) to your children, talking about them when you sit at home and when you walk along the road, when you lie down and when you get up...so that your days and the days of your children may be many.
Deuteronomy 11:19,21 NIV

Compromise makes a good umbrella but a poor roof; it is a temporary expedient.

A good man is guided by his honesty;
the evil man is destroyed by his dishonesty.
Proverbs 11:3 TLB

People who fly into a rage always make a bad landing.

The discretion of a man deferreth his anger;
and it is his glory to pass over a transgression.
Proverbs 19:11

The right train of thought can take you to a better station in life.

For as he thinks within himself, so he is.
Proverbs 23:7 NASB

135

Life was a lot simpler when we honored father and mother rather than all the major credit cards.

Children, obey your parents in the Lord, for this is right. "Honor your father and mother" — which is the first commandment with a promise — "that it may go well with you and that you may enjoy long life on the earth."
Ephesians 6:1-3 NIV

136

Smart people speak from experience — smarter people from experience, don't speak.

He who restrains his lips is wise.
Proverbs 10:19 NASB

An atheist is a man who has
no invisible means of support.

The fool hath said in his heart, There is no God.
Psalm 53:1

A half-truth is usually less than half of that.

The LORD detests lying lips, but he delights in men who are truthful.
Proverbs 12:22 NIV

❧

I make it a rule of Christian duty never to go to a place where there is not room for my Master as well as myself.

Don't be teamed with those who do not love the Lord....
How can a Christian be a partner with one who doesn't believe?
2 Corinthians 6:14,15 TLB

138

Jesus can turn water into wine, but He can't turn your whining into anything.

139

Do all things without murmurings and disputings.
Philippians 2:14

Devoting a little of yourself to
everything means committing
a great deal of yourself to nothing.

Whatsoever thy hand findeth to do, do it with thy might.
Ecclesiastes 9:10

140

The price of greatness is responsibility.

But he that is greatest among you shall be your servant.
Matthew 23:11

Obstacles are those frightful things you see when you take your eyes off the goal.

And he (Jesus) said, Come. And when Peter was come down　141
out of the ship, he walked on the water, to go to Jesus.
But when he saw the wind boisterous, he was afraid;
and beginning to sink, he cried, saying, Lord, save me.
And immediately Jesus stretched forth his hand, and caught him.
Matthew 14:29-31

A diamond is a chunk of coal that made good under pressure.

Consider it all joy...when you encounter various trials, knowing that the testing of your faith produces endurance. And let endurance have its perfect result, that you may be perfect and complete, lacking in nothing.
James 1:2-4 NASB

142

The smallest deed is better than the greatest intention!

Let us not love [merely] in theory or in speech but in deed and in truth (in practice and in sincerity).
1 John 3:18 AMP

The discipline of desire is the background of character.

*But I keep under my body, and bring it into subjection:
lest that by any means, when I have preached to others,
I myself should be a castaway.*
1 Corinthians 9:27

143

You can build a throne with bayonets, but you can't sit on it for long.

So are the ways of everyone who gains by violence;
it takes away the life of its possessors.
Proverbs 1:19 NASB

144

You can't fill an empty bucket with a dry well.

He who believes in Me, as the Scripture said,
"From his innermost being shall flow rivers of living water."
John 7:38 NASB

I've suffered a great many
catastrophes in my life.
Most of them never happened.

145

For God hath not given us the spirit of fear;
but of power, and of love, and of a sound mind.
2 Timothy 1:7

Happiness is the result of circumstances,
but joy endures in spite of circumstances.

In thy presence is fulness of joy;
at thy right hand there are pleasures for evermore.
Psalm 16:11

146

One reason the dog has so many friends:
he wags his tail instead of his tongue.

An evil man sows strife; gossip separates the best of friends.
Proverbs 16:28 TLB

What a big difference there is between giving advice and lending a hand.

Little children, let us stop just saying we love people;
let us really love them, and show it by our actions.
1 John 3:18 TLB

The man who pays an ounce of principle for a pound of popularity gets badly cheated.

For they loved the praise of men more than the praise of God.
John 12:43

The heart has no secret which our conduct does not reveal.

The good man brings good things out of the good stored up in him, and the evil man brings evil things out of the evil stored up in him.
Matthew 12:35 NIV

Guilt is concerned with the past. Worry is concerned about the future. Contentment enjoys the present.

149

Not that I am implying that I was in any personal want, for I have learned how to be content (satisfied to the point where I am not disturbed or disquieted) in whatever state I am.
Philippians 4:11 AMP

Some people are always grumbling because roses have thorns; I am thankful that thorns have roses.

Offer to God the sacrifice of thanksgiving.
Psalm 50:14 AMP

150

The next time you feel like complaining, remember that your garbage disposal probably eats better than 30 percent of the people in this world.

Let your conversation be without covetousness;
and be content with such things as ye have.
Hebrews 13:5

Our talks are often in first drafts — lots of corrections necessary!

151

For in many things we offend all. If any man offend not in word, the same is a perfect man, and able also to bridle the whole body.

James 3:2

Most of the shadows of this life are caused by standing in one's own sunshine.

A man's pride shall bring him low:
but honour shall uphold the humble in spirit.
Proverbs 29:23

152

Death is not a period but a comma in the story of life.

Jesus said unto her (Martha), I am the resurrection, and the life:
he that believeth in me, though he were dead, yet shall he live:
And whosoever liveth and believeth in me shall never die.
John 11:25,26

To know the will of God is the greatest knowledge, to find the will of God is the greatest discovery, and to do the will of God is the greatest achievement. [153]

If anyone serves Me, he must continue to follow Me
[to cleave steadfastly to Me, conform wholly to My example in
living...] and wherever I am, there will My servant be also.
If anyone serves Me, the Father will honor him.
John 12:26 AMP

People with tact have less to retract.

The heart of the righteous weighs its answers,
but the mouth of the wicked gushes evil.
Proverbs 15:28 NIV

154 # If the grass looks greener on the other side of the fence, you can bet the water bill is higher.

Let your character or moral disposition be free from love of money
[including greed, avarice, lust, and craving for earthly possessions]
and be satisfied with your present [circumstances and with what you have].
Hebrews 13:5 AMP

Being at peace with yourself is a direct result of finding peace with God.

155

And the peace of God, which passeth all understanding, shall keep your hearts and minds through Christ Jesus.
Philippians 4:7

If you want to make an easy job seem mighty hard just keep putting off doing it.

How long are ye slack to go to possess the land,
which the LORD God of your fathers hath given you?
Joshua 18:3

156

Love sees through a telescope not a microscope.

Love endures long and is patient and kind...it takes no account of
the evil done to it [it pays no attention to a suffered wrong].
1 Corinthians 13:4,5 AMP

Life is not a problem to be solved, but a gift to be enjoyed.

157

This is the day the LORD has made; let us rejoice and be glad in it.
Psalm 118:24 NIV

As I grow older, I pay less attention to what men say. I just watch what they do.

Show me your faith without deeds,
and I will show you my faith by what I do.
James 2:18 NIV

158

Some people reach the top of the ladder of success only to find it is leaning against the wrong wall.

But seek ye first the kingdom of God, and his righteousness;
and all these things shall be added unto you.
Matthew 6:33

A people that values its privileges above its principles soon loses both.

159

Uprightness and right standing with God
(moral and spiritual rectitude in every area and relation)
elevate a nation, but sin is a reproach to any people.
Proverbs 14:34 AMP

A pint of example is worth a barrelful of advice.

Brethren, join in following my example, and observe those
who walk according to the pattern you have in us.
Philippians 3:17 NASB

160

It has been my observation that most people
get ahead during the time that others waste.

The plans of the diligent lead to profit as surely as haste leads to poverty.
Proverbs 21:5 NIV

Fear makes the wolf bigger than he is.

161

Though a mighty army marches against me, my heart shall know no fear! I am confident that God will save me.
Psalm 27:3 TLB

Beware lest your footprints on the sands
of time leave only the marks of a heel.

The memory of the righteous will be a blessing,
but the name of the wicked will rot.
Proverbs 10:7 NIV

162

The happiness of every country depends
upon the character of its people,
rather than the form of its government.

Happy is that people...whose God is the LORD.
Psalm 144:15

In love, we may find it better to make allowances, rather than make points.

163

Above all, love each other deeply,
because love covers over a multitude of sins.
1 Peter 4:8 NIV

Standing in the middle of the road is
very dangerous: you get knocked down
by the traffic from both sides.

I know thy works, that thou art neither cold nor hot:
I would thou wert cold or hot.
Revelation 3:15

164

If you were given a nickname descriptive of
your character, would you be proud of it?

A good name is rather to be chosen than great riches.
Proverbs 22:1

It's easy to identify people
who can't count to ten.
They're in front of you in
the supermarket express lane.

Be patient with everyone.
1 Thessalonians 5:14 NIV

Tact is the art of making a point without making an enemy.

Reckless words pierce like a sword,
but the tongue of the wise brings healing.
Proverbs 12:18 NIV

166

Be careful of your thoughts:
They may become words at any moment.

A wise man's heart guides his mouth.
Proverbs 16:23 NIV

Fanatic: A person who's enthusiastic about something in which you have no interest.

167

Never be lacking in zeal, but keep
your spiritual fervor, serving the Lord.
Romans 12:11 NIV

It is impossible for that man to despair
who remembers that his Helper is omnipotent.

I lift up my eyes to the hills — where does my help come from?
My help comes from the LORD.... The LORD will keep you from all harm —
he will watch over your life.
Psalm 121:1,2,7 NIV

Silence is one of the hardest arguments to refute.

Whoso keepeth his mouth and his tongue keepeth his soul from troubles.
Proverbs 21:23

Anyone can hold the helm when the sea is calm.

169

If thou faint in the day of adversity, thy strength is small.
Proverbs 24:10

We learn from experience. A man never wakes up his second baby just to see it smile.

The things you have learned and received and heard and seen in me, practice these things; and the God of peace shall be with you.
Philippians 4:9 NASB

The best antique is an old friend.

Your own friend and your father's friend, forsake them not.... Better is a neighbor who is near [in spirit] than a brother who is far off [in heart].
Proverbs 27:10 AMP

Pray as if everything depended on God, and work as if everything depended upon man. 171

Faith without works is dead.
James 2:26

A good thing to remember, a better thing to do —
work with the construction gang,
not with the wrecking crew.

When you meet together, each one has a hymn, a teaching,
a disclosure of special knowledge or information.... [But] let everything
be constructive and edifying and for the good of all.
1 Corinthians 14:26 AMP

172

Money is a very excellent servant,
but a terrible master.

Command those who are rich in this present world not to be arrogant
nor to put their hope in wealth, which is so uncertain, but to put
their hope in God, who richly provides us with everything for our enjoyment.
1 Timothy 6:17 NIV

If you can't feed a hundred people then just feed one.

173

As we have therefore opportunity, let us do good unto all men.
Galatians 6:10

The trouble with stretching the truth is
that it's apt to snap back.

A false witness shall not be unpunished, and
he that speaketh lies shall not escape.
Proverbs 19:5

174

Birthdays are good for you. Statistics show
that the people who have the most live the longest.

So teach us to number our days, that we may apply our hearts unto wisdom.
Psalm 90:12

Heaven goes by favor, if it went by merit, you would stay out, and your dog would go in.

175

For it is by free grace (God's unmerited favor) that you are saved.
Ephesians 2:8 AMP

A blind man who sees is better
than a seeing man who is blind.

But blessed are your eyes, for they see: and your ears, for they hear.
Matthew 13:16

176

Men occasionally stumble over the truth,
but most of them pick themselves up and
hurry off as if nothing happened.

The ear that heareth the reproof of life abideth among the wise.
Proverbs 15:31

If the roots are deep and strong the tree needn't worry about the wind.

*Blessed is the man who trusts in the LORD.... He will be like
a tree planted by the water that sends out its roots by the stream.
It does not fear when heat comes; its leaves are always green.
It has no worries in a year of drought and never fails to bear fruit.*
Jeremiah 17:7,8 NIV

Character is much easier kept than recovered.

In speech, conduct, love, faith and purity, show yourself
an example of those who believe.
1 Timothy 4:12 NASB

178

Faults are thick where love is thin.

And above all things have fervent charity among yourselves:
for charity shall cover the multitude of sins.
1 Peter 4:8

The only way to have a friend is to be one.

179

A man that hath friends must shew himself friendly.
Proverbs 18:24

The world wants your best but God wants your all.

Thou shalt love the Lord thy God with all thy heart,
and with all thy soul, and with all thy mind.
Matthew 22:37

180

Hindsight explains the injury that
foresight would have prevented.

Do not forsake wisdom, and she will protect you.... When you walk,
your steps will not be hampered; when you run, you will not stumble.
Proverbs 4:6,12 NIV

Greatness lies not in being strong, but in the right use of strength.

181

Be strong in the Lord, and in the power of his might.
Ephesians 6:10

Do not in the darkness of night,
what you'd shun in broad daylight.

The night is far spent, the day is at hand: let us therefore cast off
the works of darkness, and let us put on the armour of light.
Romans 13:12

182

If silence is golden, not many people
can be arrested for hoarding.

In the multitude of words there wanteth not sin:
but he that refraineth his lips is wise.
Proverbs 10:19

Personality has the power to open doors, but character keeps them open.

183

The righteous shall never be removed.
Proverbs 10:30

Authority without wisdom is like a heavy axe without an edge, fitter to bruise than polish.

A ruler who lacks understanding is...a great oppressor.
Proverbs 28:16 AMP

184

Only when we have knelt before God,
can we stand before men.

Humble yourselves therefore under the mighty hand of God,
that he may exalt you in due time.
1 Peter 5:6

By perseverance the snail reached the Ark.

185

Let us run with perseverance the race marked out for us.
Hebrews 12:1 NIV

The worst moment for the atheist is when
he is really thankful and has nobody to thank.

Only a fool would say to himself, "There is no God."
Psalm 53:1 TLB

186

It is possible to be too big for God to use you but
never too small for God to use you.

A man's pride brings him low, but a man of lowly spirit gains honor.
Proverbs 29:23 NIV

Kindness gives birth to kindness.

A kind man benefits himself,
but a cruel man brings trouble on himself.
Proverbs 11:17 NIV

187

Honesty is the first chapter of the book of wisdom.

Provide things honest in the sight of all men.
Romans 12:17

188

Some minds are like finished concrete —
thoroughly mixed and permanently set.

Only by pride cometh contention: but with the well advised is wisdom.
Proverbs 13:10

It is not guided missiles, but guided morals that is our great need today.

189

The man of integrity walks securely.
Proverbs 10:9 NIV

The first rule of holes:
When you're in one, stop digging.

He lifted me out of the slimy pit...he set my feet on a rock
and gave me a firm place to stand.
Psalm 40:2 NIV

190

Deeds not stones, are the true
monuments of the great.

Let your light shine before men, that they may see your
good deeds and praise your Father in heaven.
Matthew 5:16 NIV

God always gives His best to those who leave the choice with Him.

191

Blessed be the LORD, who daily loadeth us with benefits,
even the God of our salvation.
Psalm 68:19

A Christian must keep the faith, but not to himself.

Go ye into all the world, and preach the gospel
to every creature.
Mark 16:15

192

A lot of people mistake a short memory for a clear conscience.

And herein do I exercise myself, to have always a conscience
void of offense toward God, and toward men.
Acts 24:16

Faith is not belief without proof, but trust without reservation.

193

I know whom I have believed, and am persuaded that he is able to keep that which I have committed unto him against that day.
2 Timothy 1:12

You can always tell a real friend:
When you've made a fool of yourself
he doesn't feel you've done a permanent job.

He who covers and forgives an offense seeks love, but he who
repeats or harps on a matter separates even close friends.
Proverbs 17:9 AMP

A day hemmed in prayer is less likely to unravel.

Pray about everything; tell God your needs and don't forget to thank him
for his answers. If you do this you will experience God's peace.
Philippians 4:6, TLB

Sandwich every bit of criticism between two layers of praise.

195

Correct, rebuke and encourage — with great patience and careful instruction.
2 Timothy 4:2 NIV

When you flee temptations don't leave a forwarding address.

Now flee from youthful lusts, and pursue righteousness, faith, love and peace, with those who call on the Lord from a pure heart.
2 Timothy 2:22 NASB

196

He who provides for this life, but takes no care for eternity, is wise for a moment, but a fool forever.

What is a man profited, if he shall gain the whole world, and lose his own soul?
Matthew 16:26

Morality may keep you out of jail, but it takes the blood of Jesus Christ to keep you out of hell.

197

In him we have redemption through his blood, the forgiveness of sins.
Ephesians 1:7 NIV

Courage is contagious. When a brave man takes a stand, the spines of others are stiffened.

Stand firm in the faith; be men of courage; be strong.
1 Corinthians 16:13 NIV

198

A coincidence is a small miracle where God prefers to remain anonymous.

Who can put into words and tell the mighty deeds of the Lord?
Or who can show forth all the praise [that is due Him]?
Psalm 106:2 AMP

At times, it is better to keep your mouth shut and let people wonder if you're a fool than to open it and remove all doubt. [199]

Even a fool, when he holdeth his peace, is counted wise: and he that shutteth his lips is esteemed a man of understanding.
Proverbs 17:28

Put not your trust in money,
but put your money in trust.

Trust in your money and down you go! Trust in God and flourish as a tree!
Proverbs 11:28 TLB

The man who sings his own praises
always gets the wrong pitch.

Let another man praise thee, and not thine own mouth;
a stranger, and not thine own lips.
Proverbs 27:2

Sometimes the Lord calms the storm; sometimes He lets the storm rage and calms His child.

201

And the peace of God, which transcends all understanding, will guard your hearts and your minds in Christ Jesus.
Philippians 4:7 NIV

Blame yourself as you would blame others;
excuse others as you would excuse yourself.

Therefore, however you want people to treat you, so treat them.
Matthew 7:12 NASB

202

The past should be a springboard not a hammock.

But this one thing I do, forgetting those things which are behind,
and reaching forth unto those things which are before.
Philippians 3:13

Motivation is when your dreams put on work clothes.

203

Whatever you do, work at it with all your heart,
as working for the Lord, not for men.
Colossians 3:23 NIV

Knowing and not doing are equal to not knowing at all.

Therefore, to one who knows the right thing to do,
and does not do it, to him it is sin.
James 4:17 NASB

204

Others can stop you temporarily — you are the only one who can do it permanently.

Do you not know that in a race all the runners run, but only one
gets the prize? Run in such a way as to get the prize.
1 Corinthians 9:24 NIV

The teacher asked the pupils to tell the meaning of loving-kindness. A little boy jumped up and said, "Well, if I was hungry and someone gave me a piece of bread that would be kindness. But if they put a little [205] jam on it, that would be loving-kindness."

Bless the Lord, O my soul...who crowneth thee with lovingkindness and tender mercies; Who satisfieth thy mouth with good things.
Psalm 103:1,4,5

Consider the turtle. He makes progress only when he sticks his neck out.

"Lord, if it's you," Peter replied, "tell me to come to you on the water." "Come," he (Jesus) said. Then Peter got down out of the boat, walked on the water and came toward Jesus.
Matthew 14:28,29 NIV

You can't act like a skunk without someone getting wind of it.

A good man out of the good treasure of the heart bringeth forth good things: and an evil man out of the evil treasure bringeth forth evil things.
Matthew 12:35

No man knows his true character until he has run out of gas, purchased something on the installment plan and raised an adolescent.

Consider it all joy, my brethren, when you encounter various trials, knowing that the testing of your faith produces endurance.
James 1:2,3 NASB

Laughter is a tranquilizer with no side effects.

A merry heart doeth good like a medicine.
Proverbs 17:22

It's not your outlook but your "uplook" that counts.

Behold, as the eyes of servants look unto the hand of their masters,
and as the eyes of a maiden unto the hand of her mistress;
so our eyes wait upon the LORD our God.
Psalm 123:2

208

A winner makes commitments; a loser makes promises.

LORD, who may dwell in your sanctuary?... He whose walk is blameless...who keeps his oath even when it hurts.
Psalm 15:1,2,4 NIV

It is reported that Moody's farewell words to his sons as he lay upon his deathbed were: "If God be your partner, make your plans large."

I can do all things through Christ which strengtheneth me.
Philippians 4:13

210

Faith doesn't make anything happen — faith rests on something that has happened!

My soul finds rest in God alone; my salvation comes from him.
Psalm 62:1 NIV

God never asks about our ability or our inability — just our availability.

211

I heard the voice of the Lord, saying, Whom shall I send, and who will go for us? Then said I, Here am I; send me.
Isaiah 6:8

Whenever a man is ready to uncover his sins,
God is always ready to cover them.

*He that covereth his sins shall not prosper: but whoso
confesseth and forsaketh them shall have mercy.*
Proverbs 28:13

212

Remember: The mightiest oak was once
a little nut that held its ground.

Though your beginning was insignificant, yet your end will increase greatly.
Job 8:7 NASB

What is moral is what you feel good after.

213

Blessed are the pure in heart: for they shall see God.
Matthew 5:8

Our faith should be the steering wheel
not our spare tire.

But the righteous will live by his faith.
Habakkuk 2:4 NIV

If you're heading in the wrong direction,
God allows u-turns.

If you repent, I will restore you that you may serve me.
Jeremiah 15:19 NIV

GOD'S LITTLE INSTRUCTION BOOK III

Why is it that there
is never enough time
to do a job right, but always
time enough to do it over?

217

The plans of the diligent lead surely to plenty,
but those of everyone who is hasty, surely to poverty.
Proverbs 21:5 NKJV

Prayer should be the key of the morning
and the lock of the night.

It is good to praise the LORD...to proclaim your love
in the morning and your faithfulness at night.
Psalm 92:1,2 NIV

If at first you don't succeed, try hard work.

Hard work always pays off; mere talk puts no bread on the table.
Proverbs 14:23 THE MESSAGE

It is far more impressive when others discover your good qualities without your help. 219

Let another man praise thee, and not thine own mouth; a stranger, and not thine own lips.

Proverbs 27:2

Even if you're on the right track, you'll get run over if you just sit there.

So you see, it isn't enough just to have faith. You must also do good to prove that you have it. Faith that doesn't show itself by good works is no faith at all — it is dead and useless.
James 2:17 TLB

220

Great thoughts reduced to practice become great acts.

Was not Abraham our father justified by works when he offered Isaac his son on the altar? Do you see that faith was working together with his works, and by works faith was made perfect?
James 2:21,22 NKJV

I have always thought the actions
of men the best interpreters
of their thoughts.

221

As he thinketh in his heart, so is he.
Proverbs 23:7

Keep away from people who try to belittle your ambitions. Small people always do that, but the really great people make you feel that you, too, can become great.

Blessed is the man that walketh not in the counsel of the ungodly, nor standeth in the way of sinners, nor sitteth in the seat of the scornful.
Psalm 1:1

222

Weakness of attitude becomes weakness of character.

And do not be conformed to this world, but be transformed by the renewing of your mind, that you may prove what is that good and acceptable and perfect will of God.
Romans 12:2 NKJV

Most men believe that it would
benefit them if they could get
a little from those who have more.
How much more would it benefit
them if they would learn a little
from those who know more.

223

How much better to get wisdom than gold!
Proverbs 16:16 NKJV

How much pain have cost us the evils
which have never happened!

Who of you by worrying can add a single hour to his life?
Matthew 6:27 NIV

224

You never saw a fish on the wall
with its mouth shut.

The wise in heart accept commands, but a chattering fool comes to ruin.
Proverbs 10:8 NIV

It is right to be contented
with what we have,
never with what we are.

225

I have learned how to get along happily
whether I have much or little.
Philippians 4:11 TLB

Anyone who has never made a mistake
has never tried anything new.

Forgetting what is behind and straining toward what is ahead,
I press on toward the goal.
Philippians 3:13,14 NIV

226

You see things; and you say, "Why?" But I dream
things that never were; and I say, "Why not?"

Without faith it is impossible to please God.
Hebrews 11:6 NIV

You can't hold a man down without staying down with him.

227

The man who sets a trap for others will get caught in it himself.
Proverbs 26:27 TLB

What is a cynic? A man who knows the price of everything, and the value of nothing.

The mind of sinful man is death, but the mind controlled by the Spirit is life and peace.
Romans 8:6 NIV

It is impossible to enjoy idling thoroughly unless one has plenty of work to do.

By the seventh day God had finished the work he had been doing; so on the seventh day he rested from all his work.
Genesis 2:2 NIV

Isolation is the worst possible counselor.

Where there is no counsel, the people fall;
but in the multitude of counselors there is safety.
Proverbs 11:14 NKJV

Dreaming about a thing in order to do it properly
is right; but dreaming about it when
we should be doing it is wrong.

He who gathers crops in summer is a wise son,
but he who sleeps during harvest is a disgraceful son.
Proverbs 10:5 NIV

230

I will study and prepare myself and
then someday my chance will come.

Let us not become weary in doing good, for at the proper time
we will reap a harvest if we do not give up.
Galatians 6:9 NIV

The secret to being tiresome is to tell everything.

231

Even dunces who keep quiet are thought to be wise.
Proverbs 17:28 THE MESSAGE

Every human being is intended to have
a character of his own; to be what no other is,
and to do what no other can do.

For we are His workmanship, created in Christ Jesus for good works,
which God prepared beforehand that we should walk in them.
Ephesians 2:10 NKJV

232

There is no security in life, only opportunity.

And we know that in all things God works for the good of those who love him.
Romans 8:28 NIV

A pessimist is one who makes difficulties of his opportunities; an optimist is one who makes opportunities of his difficulties.

233

If God is for us, who can be against us?
Romans 8:31 NIV

The most untutored person with passion is more persuasive than the most eloquent without.

For I know your eagerness to help...
your enthusiasm has stirred most of them to action.
2 Corinthians 9:2 NIV

234

By perseverance, the snail reached the Ark.

He who works his land will have abundant food,
but he who chases fantasies lacks judgment.
Proverbs 12:11 NIV

We can be knowledgeable without another man's knowledge, but we cannot be wise with another man's wisdom.

235

If any of you lacks wisdom, he should ask God, who gives generously to all, without finding fault, and it will be given to him.
James 1:5 NIV

A barking dog is often more useful
than a sleeping lion.

Anyone who is among the living has hope —
even a live dog is better off than a dead lion!
Ecclesiastes 9:4 NIV

One man that has a mind and knows it
can always beat ten men who haven't and don't.

I can do all things through Christ who strengthens me.
Philippians 4:13 NKJV

Chance favors prepared minds.

Wise men store up knowledge,
but the mouth of a fool invites ruin.
Proverbs 10:14 NIV

237

Sin has many tools, but a lie is
the handle which fits them all.

A lying tongue hates those it hurts, and a flattering mouth works ruin.
Proverbs 26:28 NIV

238

Don't be "consistent," but be simply true.

Simply let your "Yes" be "Yes," and your "No," "No";
anything beyond this comes from the evil one.
Matthew 5:37 NIV

It is a mistake to look
too far ahead. Only one link
of the chain of destiny
can be handled at a time.

239

You do not even know what will happen tomorrow.
What is your life? You are a mist that appears
for a little while and then vanishes.
James 4:14 NIV

There are dreamers and there are planners;
the planners make their dreams come true.

But do you not know, O foolish man, that faith without works is dead?
James 2:20 NKJV

240 Nothing is so contagious as an example. We
never do great good or great evil without bringing
about more of the same on the part of others.

Follow my example, as I follow the example of Christ.
1 Corinthians 11:1 NIV

You can make more friends in two months by becoming interested in other people than you can in two years by trying to get other people interested in you.

241

Love one another with brotherly affection [as members of one family], giving precedence and showing honor to one another.
Romans 12:10 AMP

Those who do not plan for the future
will have to live through it anyway.

Teach us to number our days aright, that we may gain a heart of wisdom.
Psalm 90:12 NIV

From what we get, we can make a living;
from what we give, however, makes a life.

One man gives freely, yet gains even more;
another withholds unduly, but comes to poverty.
Proverbs 11:24 NIV

It is better to give than to lend, and it costs about the same.

243

But love your enemies, do good to them, and lend to them without expecting to get anything back. Then your reward will be great.
Luke 6:35 NIV

A great leader never sets himself above his followers except in carrying responsibilities.

And being found in appearance as a man, he humbled himself and became obedient to death — even death on a cross!
Philippians 2:8 NIV

I don't think much of a man who is not wiser today than he was yesterday.

Study to show thyself approved unto God, a workman that needeth not to be ashamed, rightly dividing the word of truth.
2 Timothy 2:15

Live so that you wouldn't be ashamed to sell the family parrot to the town gossip.

245

What you have said in the dark will be heard in the daylight,
and what you have whispered in the ear in the inner rooms
will be proclaimed from the roofs.
Luke 12:3 NIV

The greatest pleasure in life is
doing what people say you cannot do.

For with God nothing is ever impossible.
Luke 1:37 AMP

❧

246

We have committed the Golden Rule
to memory. Let us now commit it to life.

So in everything, do to others what you would have them do to you.
Matthew 7:12 NIV

Pennies do not come from heaven — they have to be earned here on earth.

247

From the fruit of his lips a man is filled with good things as surely as the work of his hands rewards him.
Proverbs 12:14 NIV

Diligence is the greatest of teachers.

Keep thy heart with all diligence; for out of it are the issues of life.
Proverbs 4:23

There is no royal road to anything. One thing at a time, and all things in succession. That which grows slowly endures.

248

We do not want you to become lazy, but to imitate those
who through faith and patience inherit what has been promised.
Hebrews 6:12 NIV

Patience serves as a protection against wrongs as clothes do against cold. For if you put on more clothes as the cold increases, it will have no power to hurt you. So in like manner you must grow in patience when you meet with great wrongs, and they will be powerless to vex you.

249

But let patience have her perfect work,
that ye may be perfect and entire, wanting nothing.
James 1:4

Here is the test to find whether your mission on earth is finished: If you're alive, it isn't.

For as the days of a tree, so will be the days of my people;
my chosen ones will long enjoy the works of their hands.
Isaiah 65:22 NIV

250

The greatest mistake you can make in life is to be continually fearing you will make one.

Be strong and courageous. Do not be afraid or terrified because of them, for
the LORD your God goes with you; he will never leave you nor forsake you.
Deuteronomy 31:6 NIV

You have reached the pinnacle of success as soon as you become uninterested in money, compliments, or publicity.

251

Do nothing out of selfish ambition or vain conceit,
but in humility consider others better than yourselves.
Philippians 2:3 NIV

Try not to become a man of success,
but rather a man of virtue.

A good name is more desirable than great riches;
to be esteemed is better than silver or gold.
Proverbs 22:1 NIV

252

Let no feeling of discouragement prey upon you,
and in the end you are sure to succeed.

The LORD himself goes before you and will be with you; he will never
leave you nor forsake you. Do not be afraid; do not be discouraged.
Deuteronomy 31:8 NIV

Men are not influenced by things, but by their thoughts about things.

253

Finally, brothers, whatever is true, whatever is noble, whatever is right, whatever is pure, whatever is lovely, whatever is admirable — if anything is excellent or praiseworthy — think about such things.
Philippians 4:8 NIV

Short as life is, we make it still shorter
by the careless waste of time.

Man is like a breath; his days are like a fleeting shadow.
Psalm 144:4 NIV

254

Vision is the art of seeing things invisible.

By faith he [Abraham] left Egypt, not fearing the king's anger;
he persevered because he saw him who is invisible.
Hebrews 11:27 NIV

Wisdom begins with sacrifice of immediate pleasures for long-range purposes.

255

Make level paths for your feet and take only ways that are firm.
Do not swerve to the right or to the left; keep your foot from evil.
Proverbs 4:26,27 NIV

Study without reflection is a waste of time; reflection without study is dangerous.

Do not let this Book of the Law depart from your mouth; meditate on it day and night, so that you may be careful to do everything written in it. Then you will be prosperous and successful.
Joshua 1:8 NIV

256

To know is not to be wise.... There is no fool so great a fool as a knowing fool. But to know how to use knowledge is to have wisdom.

The fear of the LORD is the beginning of knowledge, but fools despise wisdom and discipline.
Proverbs 1:7 NIV

Better to light a candle than to curse the darkness.

257

The eye is the lamp of the body. If your eyes are good, your whole body will be full of light.
Matthew 6:22 NIV

What comes with ease, goes with ease.

Dishonest money dwindles away, but he who
gathers money little by little makes it grow.
Proverbs 13:11 NIV

258 Render more service than that for which you are paid and you will soon be paid for more than you render. This is *The law of increasing returns.*

Remember this: Whoever sows sparingly will also reap sparingly,
and whoever sows generously will also reap generously.
2 Corinthians 9:6 NIV

Those who complain the most usually work the least.

259

Do everything without complaining or arguing.
Philippians 2:14 NIV

We cannot be guilty of a greater act of uncharitableness, than to interpret the afflictions which befall our neighbors, as punishment and judgments.

Stop judging by mere appearances, and make a right judgment.
John 7:24 NIV

260   Aspiration shows us the goal and the distance to it; inspiration encourages with a view of how far we have come. Aspiration gives us the map of the journey; inspiration furnishes the music to keep us marching.

Then the LORD answered me and said, "Record the vision and inscribe it on tablets, that the one who reads it may run."
Habakkuk 2:2 NASB

Understanding is the reward of faith. Therefore seek not to understand that thou mayest believe, but believe that thou mayest understand.

261

Jesus answered, "The work of God is this: to believe in the one he has sent." John 6:29 NIV

Amid the greatest difficulties of my Administration, when I could not see any other resort, I would place my whole reliance in God, knowing that all would go well, and that He would decide for the right.

Cast your cares on the LORD and he will sustain you.
Psalm 55:22 NIV

262

A true friend never gets in your way unless you happen to be going down.

If one falls down, his friend can help him up. But pity
the man who falls and has no one to help him up!
Ecclesiastes 4:10 NIV

Other books were given for our information, the Bible was given for our transformation.

263

Do not conform any longer to the pattern of this world,
but be transformed by the renewing of your mind.
Romans 12:2 NIV

We must adjust to changing times
and still hold to unchanging principles.

The word of the Lord stands forever.
1 Peter 1:25 NIV

264

The seen is the changing,
the unseen is the unchanging.

So we fix our eyes not on what is seen, but on what is unseen.
For what is seen is temporary, but what is unseen is eternal.
2 Corinthians 4:18 NIV

The trouble with modern civilization is that we so often mistake respectability for character.

Man looks at the outward appearance,
but the LORD looks at the heart.
1 Samuel 16:7 NIV

One of the disconcerting facts about the spiritual life is that God takes you at your word.

Whatever your lips utter you must be sure to do, because you made your vow freely to the LORD your God with your own mouth.
Deuteronomy 23:23 NIV

266

Kindness has converted more people than zeal, science, or eloquence.

Or do you show contempt for the riches of his kindness, tolerance and patience, not realizing that God's kindness leads you toward repentance?
Romans 2:4 NIV

A quiet conscience
sleeps in thunder.

267

Paul looked straight at the Sanhedrin and said, "My brothers,
I have fulfilled my duty to God in all good conscience to this day."
Acts 23:1 NIV

Conformity is the jailer of freedom
and the enemy of growth.

Then you will know the truth, and the truth will set you free.
John 8:32 NIV

All too often a clear conscience is merely
the result of a bad memory.

These liars have lied so well and for so long that
they've lost their capacity for truth.
1 Timothy 4:2 THE MESSAGE

Courage is rightly esteemed the first of human qualities, because...it is the quality which guarantees all others.

269

Be strong and courageous...for the Lord your God will be with you wherever you go.
Joshua 1:9 NIV

Courage is never to let your actions be
influenced by your fears.

For God has not given us a spirit of fear,
but of power and of love and of a sound mind.
2 Timothy 1:7 NKJV

270

Despair is the sin which cannot find —
because it will not look for it — forgiveness.

If we confess our sins, he is faithful and just and will forgive us
our sins and purify us from all unrighteousness.
1 John 1:9 NIV

There are enough targets to aim at without firing at each other.

271

Be kind and compassionate to one another,
forgiving each other, just as in Christ God forgave you.
Ephesians 4:32 NIV

You always pass failure on the way to success.

And we know that all things work together for good to those who love God, to those who are the called according to His purpose.
Romans 8:28 NKJV

❧

272

There is nothing final about a mistake, except its being taken as final.

The steps of a good man are ordered by the LORD....
Though he fall, he shall not be utterly cast down.
Psalm 37:23,24

We are never defeated unless we give up on God.

273

In all these things we are more than conquerors through him who loved us.
Romans 8:37 NIV

Faith furnishes prayer with wings,
without which it cannot soar to Heaven.

Whatever you ask for in prayer, believe that you
have received it, and it will be yours.
Mark 11:24 NIV

274 Faith is not a dam which prevents the flow of
the river of reason and thought; it is a levee which
prevents unreason from flooding the countryside.

Without weakening in his faith, he [Abraham] faced
the fact that his body was as good as dead.
Romans 4:19 NIV

An ounce of parent is worth a pound of the clergy.

Train a child in the way he should go,
and when he is old he will not turn from it.
Proverbs 22:6 NIV

Hope arouses, as nothing else can arouse,
a passion for the possible.

Praise be to the God and Father of our Lord Jesus Christ!
In his great mercy he has given us new birth into a living hope
through the resurrection of Jesus Christ from the dead.
1 Peter 1:3 NIV

276

It is the heart that is not yet sure of its God
that is afraid to laugh in His presence.

Let us then approach the throne of grace with confidence, so that
we may receive mercy and find grace to help us in our time of need.
Hebrews 4:16 NIV

Marriage is that relation between man and woman in which the independence is equal, the dependence mutual, and the obligation reciprocal.

277

Wives, understand and support your husbands....
Husbands, go all out in love for your wives.
Colossians 3:18,19 THE MESSAGE

The goal in marriage is not to think alike, but to think together.

For this reason a man will leave his father and mother
and be united to his wife, and the two will become one flesh.
Ephesians 5:31 NIV

Money \ 'me-ne \ n, A blessing that is of no advantage to us excepting when we part with it.

Each man should give what he has decided in his heart to give,
not reluctantly or under compulsion, for God loves a cheerful giver.
2 Corinthians 9:7 NIV

Obedience is the "virtue-making virtue."

279

Does the LORD delight in burnt offerings and sacrifices as much as in obeying the voice of the Lord? To obey is better than sacrifice.
1 Samuel 15:22 NIV

All sunshine makes a desert.

Consider it pure joy, my brothers, whenever you face trials of many kinds, because you know that the testing of your faith develops perseverance.
James 1:2,3 NIV

Patience is the companion of wisdom.

Let us run with patience the race that is set before us.
Hebrews 12:1

If I had eight hours to chop down a tree, I'd spend six sharpening my ax. 281

Be prepared in season and out of season.
2 Timothy 4:2 NIV

What is the use of praying if at the very moment of prayer we have so little confidence in God that we are busy planning our own kind of answer to our prayer?

Do not be anxious about anything, but in everything, by prayer and petition, with thanksgiving, present your requests to God.
Philippians 4:6 NIV

282

Our motive for prayer must be the divine will, not our own.

Therefore do not be foolish, but understand what the Lord's will is.
Ephesians 5:17 NIV

I do not feel obliged to believe
that the same God who
has endowed us with sense,
reason, and intellect has
intended us to forgo their use.

283

Each one should be fully convinced in his own mind.
Romans 14:5 NIV

Self-reform is the answer to world-reform.

Each of us will give an account of himself to God.
Romans 14:12 NIV

The worst cliques are those which consist of one man.

Do not think of yourself more highly than you ought.
Romans 12:3 NIV

In taking revenge a man is but even with his enemy; but in passing it over, he is superior.

285

Do not repay anyone evil for evil. Be careful to do what is right in the eyes of everybody.
Romans 12:17 NIV

Let not the nation count wealth as wealth;
let it count righteousness as wealth.

Blessed is the nation whose God is the LORD.
Psalm 33:12 NIV

286

The secrets of success are a good wife
and a steady job. My wife told me.

He who finds a wife finds what is good and receives favor from the LORD.
Proverbs 18:22 NIV

The power of a man's virtue should not be measured by his special efforts, but by his ordinary doing.

287

Live such good lives among the pagans that, though they accuse you of doing wrong, they may see your good deeds and glorify God.
1 Peter 2:12 NIV

In this world it is not what we take up,
but what we give up, that makes us rich.

*Give, and it will be given to you. A good measure, pressed down,
shaken together and running over, will be poured into your lap.*
Luke 6:38 NIV

288
It is not a crime to be rich, nor a virtue to be
poor.... The sin lies in hoarding wealth and
keeping it from circulating freely to all who need it.

*You will be made rich in every way so that you can be generous on
every occasion...your generosity will result in thanksgiving to God.*
2 Corinthians 9:11 NIV

The created world is but a small parenthesis in eternity.

So we fix our eyes not on what is seen, but on what is unseen.
For what is seen is temporary, but what is unseen is eternal.
2 Corinthians 4:18 NIV

Money is like promises — easier made than kept.

Whoever trusts in his riches will fall,
but the righteous will thrive like a green leaf.
Proverbs 11:28 NIV

Money is of no value; it cannot spend itself.
All depends on the skill of the spender.

Moreover it is required in stewards that one be found faithful.
1 Corinthians 4:2 NKJV

The squeaky wheel doesn't always get greased; it often gets replaced.

291

Let your conversation be always full of grace, seasoned with salt, so that you may know how to answer everyone.
Colossians 4:6 NIV

No generalization is wholly true, not even this one.

My mouth speaks what is true, for my lips detest wickedness.
Proverbs 8:7 NIV

292

If thou thinkest twice, before thou speakest once, thou wilt speak twice the better for it.

He who guards his mouth and his tongue keeps himself from calamity.
Proverbs 21:23 NIV

The drops of rain make a hole in the stone not by violence but by oft falling.

293

Through patience a ruler can be persuaded,
and a gentle tongue can break a bone.
Proverbs 25:15 NIV

Our grand business in life is not to see
what lies dimly at a distance,
but to do what lies clearly at hand.

Whatever your hand finds to do, do it with all your might.
Ecclesiastes 9:10 NIV

294

The world is moving so fast these days
that the man who says it can't be done is
generally interrupted by someone doing it.

For nothing is impossible with God.
Luke 1:37 NIV

Every tomorrow has two handles. You can take hold of the handle of anxiety or the handle of enthusiasm. Upon your choice so will be the day.

295

In the morning, O LORD, you hear my voice; in the morning I lay my requests before you and wait in expectation.
Psalm 5:3 NIV

The last of the human freedoms is to choose one's attitude in any given set of circumstances.

Whatever is true...noble...right...pure...lovely...admirable...
excellent or praiseworthy — think about such things.
Philippians 4:8 NIV

296

Example is not the main thing in influencing others. It is the only thing.

Christ suffered for you, leaving you an example,
that you should follow in his steps.
1 Peter 2:21 NIV

Genius is nothing but a greater aptitude for patience.

297

Imitate those who through faith and patience inherit what has been promised.
Hebrews 6:12 NIV

Blessed is the man who, having nothing to say,
abstains from giving in words evidence of the fact.

The tongue is a small part of the body, but it makes great boasts.
Consider what a great forest is set on fire by a small spark.
James 3:5 NIV

Most of man's trouble comes from
his inability to be still.

Be still, and know that I am God; I will be exalted among the nations,
I will be exalted in the earth.
Psalm 46:10 NIV

I don't know why we are in such a hurry to get up when we fall down. You might think we would lie there and rest awhile. [299]

He makes me lie down in green pastures,
he leads me beside quiet waters, he restores my soul.
Psalm 23:2,3

Happiness is a dividend on a well-invested life.

When you eat the labor of your hands, you shall be happy,
and it shall be well with you.
Psalm 128:2 NKJV

❧

300

I am not interested in the past.
I am interested in the future, for that is where
I expect to spend the rest of my life.

Forgetting what is behind and straining toward what is ahead,
I press on toward the goal to win the prize.
Philippians 3:13,14 NIV

The future is something which everyone reaches at a rate of sixty minutes an hour, whatever he does, whoever he is. [301]

For the revelation awaits an appointed time; it speaks of the end and will not prove false. Though it linger, wait for it; it will certainly come and will not delay.
Habakkuk 2:3 NIV

A person may sometimes have a clear conscience
simply because his head is empty.

In the last times some in the church will turn away from Christ...
their consciences won't even bother them.
1 Timothy 4:1,2 TLB

A wise man sometimes changes his mind,
but a fool never.

The way of a fool seems right to him, but a wise man listens to advice.
Proverbs 12:15 NIV

A leader is a dealer in hope.

*A faith and knowledge resting on the
hope of eternal life, which God, who does not
lie, promised before the beginning of time.*
Titus 1:2 NIV

We don't need any more leadership training;
we need some followership training.

Anyone who does not take his cross and follow me is not worthy of me.
Matthew 10:38 NIV

304

Any plant growing in the wrong place is a "weed."

But in fact God has arranged the parts in the body,
every one of them, just as he wanted them to be.
1 Corinthians 12:18 NIV

The well of Providence is deep. It's the buckets we bring to it that are small.

305

Look at the birds of the air...your heavenly Father feeds them.
Are you not much more valuable than they?
Matthew 6:26 NIV

Whatever you dislike in another person take care to correct in yourself.

Why do you look at the speck of sawdust in your brother's eye and pay no attention to the plank in your own eye?
Matthew 7:3 NIV

Honor's a lease for life to come.

We are looking forward to a new heaven and a new earth, the home of righteousness.
2 Peter 3:13 NIV

Hope is brightest when it dawns from fears.

He has delivered us from such a deadly peril,
and he will deliver us. On him we have set our hope
that he will continue to deliver us.
2 Corinthians 1:10 NIV

307

Any man may commit a mistake,
but none but a fool will continue in it.

Though a righteous man falls seven times, he rises again,
but the wicked are brought down by calamity.
Proverbs 24:16 NIV

Gold is the fool's curtain,
which hides all his defects from the world.

The wealth of the rich is their fortified city;
they imagine it an unscalable wall.
Proverbs 18:11 NIV

Conversation is the vent of character as well as of thought.

For out of the overflow of the heart the mouth speaks.
The good man brings good things out of the good stored up in him,
and the evil man brings evil things out of the evil stored up in him.
Matthew 12:34,35 NIV

309

Every individual has a place to fill in the world,
and is important, in some respect,
whether he chooses to be so or not.

For I know the thoughts and plans that I have for you, says the Lord,
thoughts and plans for welfare and peace and not for evil,
to give you hope in your final outcome.
Jeremiah 29:11 AMP

310

Goodness is the only investment that never fails.

But the fruit of the Spirit is love, joy, peace, patience, kindness, goodness,
faithfulness, gentleness, self-control; against such things there is no law.
Galatians 5:22,23 NASB

It is what we give up, not what we lay up, that adds to our lasting store.

311

Do not store up for yourselves treasures on earth....
But store up for yourselves treasures in heaven....
For where your treasure is, there your heart will be also.
Matthew 6:19-21 NIV

The time to repair the roof is when the sun is shining.

312 *Go to the ant...consider its ways and be wise! It has no commander...
yet it stores its provisions in summer and gathers its food at harvest.*
Proverbs 6:6, 8 NIV

The men who try to do something and fail are infinitely better than those who try nothing and succeed.

313

Take the thousand and give it to the one who risked the most. And get rid of this "play-it-safe" who won't go out on a limb. Matthew 25:29,30 THE MESSAGE

No worldly success can compensate for failure in the home.

Children, obey your parents in the Lord, for this is right....
And you, fathers, do not provoke your children to wrath,
but bring them up in the training and admonition of the Lord.
Ephesians 6:1,4 NKJV

314

Coming together is a beginning; keeping together is progress; working together is success.

How good and pleasant it is when brothers live together in unity!...
For there the LORD bestows his blessing, even life forevermore.
Psalm 133:1,3 NIV

If the journey is long, take only the necessities. This leaves room to acquire the luxuries along the way.

315

Do not store up for yourselves treasures on earth, where moth and rust destroy, and where thieves break in and steal.
Matthew 6:19 NIV

Time is a great teacher, but unfortunately it kills all its pupils.

Take my yoke upon you and learn from me, for I am gentle and humble in heart, and you will find rest for your souls.
Matthew 11:29 NIV

316

Once the game is over, the king and the pawn go back into the same box.

For all can see that wise men die; the foolish and the senseless alike perish and leave their wealth to others.
Psalm 49:10 NIV

Unless otherwise indicated, all Scripture quotations are taken from the *King James Version* of the Bible.

Some quotes are taken from *The New International Version*® NIV.® Copyright © 1973, 1978, 1984 by International Bible Society. Used by permission of Zondervan Publishing House. All rights reserved.

Scripture quotations marked NKJV are taken from *The New King James Version* of the Bible. Copyright © 1979, 1980, 1982, 1994 by Thomas Nelson, Inc., Publishers. Used by permission.

Verses marked THE MESSAGE are taken from *The Message*, Eugene Peterson (Colorado Springs, CO: NavPress, 1993, 1994, 1995), pp. 893, 902, 522, 504, 76.

317

Verses marked TLB are taken from *The Living Bible*, copyright © 1971. Used by permission of Tyndale House Publishers, Inc., Wheaton, Illinois 60189. All rights reserved.

Scripture quotations marked AMP are taken from *The Amplified Bible, Old Testament* copyright © 1965, 1987 by Zondervan Publishing House, Grand Rapids, Michigan. *New Testament* copyright © 1958, 1987 by The Lockman Foundation, La Habra, California. Used by permission.

Scripture quotations marked NASB are taken from the *New American Standard Bible*. Copyright © The Lockman Foundation, 1960, 1962, 1963, 1968, 1971, 1973, 1975, 1977. Used by permission.

We acknowledge and thank the following people for the quotes used in this book:

Addison, Joseph 260, Anspacher, Louis, K. 277, Arabian Proverb 248,258,302,280, Ash, Mary Kay 195, Ashe, Arthur 242, Augustine, St. 261,280, Bach, Richard 250, Bagehot, Walter 246, Ball, Ivern 202, Ballou, Hosea 311, Barnum, P.T. 172, Baruch, Bernard 124, Battista, Dr.O.A. 127, Orlando, A. 251, Beecher, Henry Ward 181,288, Bender, Morris 123, Berger, Sally 224, Berloiz, Hector 316, Bierce, Ambrose 278, Billings, Josh 168,290 Boetcker, William J.H. 223, Bonaparte, Napoleon 303, Bottome, Phyllis 272, Bradstreet, Anne 184, Browne, Thomas 289, Buchan, John 137, Buscaglia, Leo 163, Butler, Samuel 306, Carlyle, Thomas 294, Carnegie, Andrew 158, Carnegie, Dale 241, Carroll, Maureen 304, Carter, Jimmy 264, Chambers, Oswald 230, Channing 232, Chinese Proverb 257, Churchill, Sir Winston 140,176,239,269 Cicero, Marcus 308, Climacus, St. John 274, Coffin, William Sloane Jr. 276, Confucius 256,286, Cooke, Alistair 126, Cox, Mercelene 208, Day, Dorothy 266, Dickens, Charles 128, Dodds, Robert C. 278, Dooey, Joseph P. 157, Drucker, Peter 120, Eastman, Max 299, Einstein, Albert 222,252, Eisenberg, Larry 126, Eisenhower, Dwight D. 159, Eliot, George 298, Elliott, Jim 191, Emerson, Ralph Waldo 119,152,179,290,309, Exley, Richard 121, Farmer's Almanac 304, Farr, Charles 130, Farver, Amos J. 152, Feather, William 218, Feltham, Owen 218,308, Fillmore, Charles 288, Fintelstein, Louis 255, Fisher, Len 242, Ford, Henry 160, Ford, George W. 189, Ford, Henry 314, Franki, Victor 296, Franklin, Benjamin 297, Freeman 118, Fuller, Thomas 267,285, Fusdick, Harry Emerson 294, Galileo 283, Gibbs, Philip 243, Glasgow, Arnold S. 116, Glasgow, Arnold H. 153,262, Graham, Billy 198, Haliburton, Thomas Chandler 162, Hawthorne 310, Haye, George J. 279, Hazlitt, William 220, Hemingway, Ernest 213, Henderson, June 165, Hill, Napolian 258, Holland, J.G. 248, Holmes, Oliver Wendell 114,200,238,292, Howell, James 178, Hubbard, Elbert G. 250, Hugo, Victor 254, Irving, Washington 236, Italian Proverb 316, Ivins, Molly 190, Jefferson, Thomas 188,224, Jerome, Jerome K. 228, Jones, Llyod 313, Kennedy, John F. 268,312, Kerr, Alphonse 150,

318

Kettering, Charles F. 300, Keyes, Jr.,Ken S. 115, Koestler, Arthur 270, Koop, C. Everett 133, Larson, Doug 120,192,206, LeBoeuf, Michael 140,144, Letterman, Elmer G. 132, Lewis,C.,S. 301, Lincoln, Abraham 230,244,252,262,281, Locke, John 143,221, Lorenzoni, Rev. Larry 174, Lowell, James Russell 134, Lucretius 293, Macdonald, George 276, MacKintosh, Sir James 225, Mansell, Reginald 233, MarKham, Edwin 246, Martin, Judith S. 219, Mason, John 208, McKenzie, E.C. 182, Merton, Thomas 282, Miklas, Sebastian 284, Miller Olin 155, Montaigne, Michel de 235, Moody, Dwight L. 210, Moore, Hannah 141, Motley, John Lothrop 190, Nemerov, Howard 286, Newton, John 138, Nimeth, Albert J. 167, Olson, Jon 166, Orben, Robert 136, Orbin, Robert 150, Ormont, Jules 244, Paine, Thomas 178, Pascal, Blaise 287,298, Pasteur, Louis 237, Patrick, Jim 192, Peale, Norman Vincent 124, Peers, John 291, Penn, William 292, Peter, Lawrence J. 194, Pictetus, E. 253, Plato 264, Reagan, Ronald 273, Robinson, Parkes 203, Rochefoucauld, Francois de La 234,240, Rogers, Will 134,220,245, Rooney, Mickey 272, Roosevelt, Theodore 271, Rossetti, Dante Gabriel 186, Sackman, Ralph W. 260, Schweitzer, Albert 296, Scott, Sir Walter 307, Scupoli, D. Lavrence 282, Shaw, George Bernard 226,236,284, Sheen, Fulton J. 274, Sinclair, James S. 199, Smith, Malcolm 210, Sockman, Ralph W. 302, Spanish Proverb 275, Spellman, Cardinal Francis J. 171, Sprat, Thomas 306, Spurgeon, Charles 182,185,197,234,256, Steele, Mark 139, Stuart, Duncan 300, Swift, Jonathan 254, Syrus, Dublilius 169, Taylor, J. Hudson, 122, Taylor, Jeremy 168, Teresa, Mother 173,266, Thatcher, Margaret 164,247, Tillotson, John 196, Tjingaete, Fanuel 209, Trueblood, Elton 193, Twain, Mark 131,145,175,222,232, Tweedsmuir, Lord 137, Unamuno, Miguel de 229, Vinci, Leonardo da 249, Voltaire, Francois 231, Walker, Mort 116, Washington, Booker T. 114,227, Waterloo, Anthonie 147, Webb, Mary 305, Wilde, Oscar 228, Williams, Bern 138, Williams, Grace 170, Workman, Lorene 204,207, Yeltsin, Boris 144, Zeller, Hubert van 270, Ziglar, Zig 204.

Additional copies of this book and other titles in the *God's Little Instruction Book Series* are available at your local bookstore.

God's Little Instruction Book for Mom

God's Little Instruction Book for Dad

God's Little Instruction Book for Graduates

God's Little Instruction Book for Students

God's Little Instruction Book for Kids

God's Little Instruction Book for Couples

God's Little Instruction Book for Men

God's Little Instruction Book on Character

God's Little Instruction Book on Success

God's Little Instruction Book on Friendship

God's Little Instruction Book on Love

God's Little Instruction Book on Prayer

God's Little Instruction Book for New Believers

Honor Books, Inc.

45, Box 55388

Tulsa, OK 74155